James

MacKeown

James MacKeown

The Art of Living

by

Andrew Lambirth

Foreword by

Brian Kennedy

First Published 2003

Preface
Myles Pepper

Introduction
Brian Kennedy

Main Text
Andrew Lambirth

Paintings and Drawings
James MacKeown

Book Design
David Craven

Printed in Wales at
Gomer Press

ISBN 0 9536108 4 5

This book is published in Wales by Myles Pepper, Director,
West Wales Arts Centre, 16 West Street,Fishguard, Pembrokeshire SA65 9AE. Tele / Fax 01348 873867,
email: westwalesart@btconnect.com website:http//btconnect. com/WEST-WALES-ARTS/

Cover detail of James MacKeown Self Portrait

Contents

Preface

James MacKeown has been represented by the gallery since its inception and therefore we are even more delighted to be featuring the work of this outstanding artist as we celebrate our twentieth anniversary.

In this publication MacKeown features the nude, landscapes and domestic scenes of his everyday family life and given that we have known each other for almost thirty years his family scenes are of particularly great interest and meaning to me, but they are not in any way what one might call sentimental works, far from it – they are works of a painter who can now consider himself established.

Myles Pepper
West Wales Arts Centre

Foreword

I have admired the work of James MacKeown for a good number of years. I first recall seeing it in his one-man exhibition held at Grant Fine Art in Newcastle, County Down, in June 1981 and again, at the same venue, a couple of years later. These events remain clear in my mind, for MacKeown's grandfather, the celebrated Ulster painter Tom Carr, lived and worked in Newcastle from the early 1940s till the 1950s and continued to draw his inspiration from that area for decades thereafter. Later, my wife and I settled in the village of Seaforde, just a few miles from Newcastle, and still in the summer time I see people bathing in the sea there, eating an ice cream, chatting over a country fence or tending sheep and cattle, just as Tom Carr observed them in the '40s and later. Moreover, for a brief time I was taught by Tom Carr while studying at the Belfast College of Art in the 1960s, so his themes and subject matter are part of my own consciousness of the place where I live. This consciousness is heightened, too, by a good friend and neighbour who has one of MacKeown's beach scenes hanging just inside his front door.

But this is not to define James MacKeown's art in terms of his grandfather's, although to my generation living in Ulster there is much in common between them. Perhaps this is also due in part to the loose thread of Sickert, Camden Town and Euston Road that runs between them although where Carr remained an observer of events, MacKeown, as Andrew Lambirth says, is more assertively an *intimiste* in the tradition of Vuillard. For me Velázquez, in pictures like the 'Rokeby Venus', also comes to mind, in, for example, a MacKeown nude lying on a bed, half seen from behind through a doorway, or the disturbed privacy of a women dressing, all of which lend a suggestion of intrusion on the part of the viewer. This business of intruding, of not quite belonging, is in part, too, the situation of one living in a foreign land and with MacKeown—an Irishman domiciled in France—one is always conscious of 'place', of a continual transference between one home and another. Thus we find at the heart of his art everyday situations made pregnant with memory and association and, most of all, life.

I shall continue to admire MacKeown's painting and the gentleness that it epitomizes, a land of calm and humanity amid a world of hype and bombast. I shall continue to look forward, as I always do, to visiting my neighbour, to passing by his 'MacKeown' and to our chat, putting to rights a dizzy world.

S. B. Kennedy
Ulster Museum

'TREES IN THE GREEN FIELD' Oil on Canvas

'PATH TO THE BEACH' Oil on Canvas

James MacKeown: The Art of Living

James MacKeown paints the things around him: the rooms and landscapes, the people and the objects, the daily rituals of living. His work is autobiographical, but not intensely so. Although it can be seen as a celebration of the act of living, it also has strong abstract impulses which qualify it for consideration as art made as a formal investigation of light, colour, line and volume.

Art is a way of making sense of life. A serious illness ten years ago, coupled with the recent deaths of his grandfather and father, have confronted MacKeown with the issues of life and death. Art has always concerned itself with the great verities, and although not every painting is intended as a *memento mori,* every real painting is nevertheless an engagement with the values that bind our existence. MacKeown's paintings are not moralizing statements about how to live your life, but his sharpened awareness of the human condition has had the effect of deepening the emotional substructure of his art. Through his paintings he is seeking the right response - which inevitably tends to operate on different levels: emotional, aesthetic, formal. Thus his art is about celebration, but it is also about memory, and at the same time, it is profoundly about paint.

A Brief Biography

James MacKeown was born in 1961 just outside London, but regards himself as Irish, Celtic. His grandfather was the distinguished Ulster painter Tom Carr (1909-99) who studied at the Slade in the late 1920s, personally knew Sickert and Wilson Steer and became closely associated with that bunch of painters including William Coldstream, Victor Pasmore and Claude Rogers, who were to become known as the Euston Road Group. Carr, a fully-paid-up member of this particular avant-garde, contributed to the pioneering cul-de-sac of an exhibition, *Objective Abstractions,* in 1934. Along with such luminaries as Pasmore, Geoffrey Tibble and Rodrigo Moynihan, he exhibited youthful attempts at abstraction which showed more enthusiasm than real understanding. (Even Pasmore admitted later that he didn't really know what he was doing then, and swiftly returned to a Bonnard- and Whistler-inflected realism before finally converting to abstraction in 1947.)

For Carr it was a time of experiment, a useful phase in his development, which bequeathed him a greater understanding of pictorial structure. By temperament, he had more in common with the British tradition of robust realism exemplified by the Camden Town Group, than with the formal developments of European Modernism. It is a tradition which has worn well and which is still full of sap and resonance. A situation assisted by the fact that Carr's grandson James MacKeown has sprung from it and continues to uphold it with inventiveness and fidelity.

With the outbreak of the Second World War, Carr decided to give up his London life, his regular shows at the Redfern and other West End galleries, and dispense with all avant-garde associations. (It is for this reason that he features only in the first half of 'The Townsend Journals - An Artist's Record of His Times 1928-51'.) To all intents and purposes he dropped out. He moved to Newcastle, Co Down, and used his old abstract paintings to line and waterproof his beehives. His grandson visited him frequently and as a boy worked beside him in the studio.

MacKeown's childhood was divided between Ireland, East Anglia, Turkey and Wales. There were French interludes also. His family has known his French wife's family for many years. When they were children, James and his wife Marie were sent on exchange - he to France, she to England - to learn the language. She was 11, he was 14. (It was a formative period in other respects, for it was at this point that MacKeown discovered oil paint). Boy and girl grew up and went their separate ways, and in the fullness of time MacKeown married a Welsh girl, by whom he had a daughter. Years later he re-met Marie, they married, and settled in the very place James had stayed as a boy learning French. The pattern is remarkable.

Education was haphazard. A peripatetic existence does not make for settled schooling, and feeling the need for a period of extended study, the nineteen-year-old MacKeown took an Open University course in the Humanities. Naturally he considered attending art school, but he allowed himself to be dissuaded. 'I was accepted onto two Foundation courses - at Belfast and Camberwell. I met Dick Lee (then running the painting school at Camberwell) and discussed what I was going to achieve by doing Foundation. Then I saw Bill Coldstream, because I thought the Slade would be the place to go, but he just said "you don't need to go to the Slade, you won't learn anything". It was really quite funny. So I didn't go. A couple of years afterwards I wondered whether I should have gone, but I don't regret it now at all. I was already beginning to show, and although it did take me a long time to find what I wanted in painting, it was a way of finding that agreed with me a lot.'

MacKeown has been living near Etretat in Normandy since 1988, which means that he has lived longer in France than in any other country. Maupassant called the distinctive rock formation of the Etretat cliffs, painted by so many artists from Courbet to Hockney, 'The Elephant', because of its trunk-like outline. MacKeown, the francophile Irishman, chooses less obvious, more intimate subjects than The Elephant, working steadily away to capture something of his sense of pleasure in things seen. He is an *intimiste* in the tradition of Vuillard, yet there is also an unavoidable comparison with Sickert, who spent so much of his time in Dieppe, and who also had a passion for painting figures in interiors (also beaches and the patterns made by the play and fall of light).

The resolute structuring, at times gentled by colour, at times reinforced by it, which distinguishes his art, lies at the heart of his approach to painting. The vertical/horizontal axes of a window painting, for instance, in which the angles of curtain and sill and frame seem almost to square up the image, as if for transfer to a larger format. Or the strong horizontals of breakers and beach. Or the vertical framing of a view through a doorway into bedroom or bathroom. MacKeown favours asymmetrical compositions and chalky textures, and constantly re-works a subject. He is vigilant in his pursuit of perfection.

'SELF PORTRAIT' Mixed Media

People

From the very earliest years of thinking about art, MacKeown always wanted to paint people, and they still constitute a large and consistent element of his total subject matter. It is not always his wife who appears in these pictures - MacKeown usually has a choice of four models to call upon, besides his numerous children, but it is essential that he knows the sitter well, or he is unable to bring to his depiction the requisite fluency of observation. He starts by drawing a model, or by making a head study in paint. He needs to know a sitter for at least three or four months before embarking upon a big picture.

Familiarity is crucial to MacKeown's methods of working, but a degree of surprise, even novelty, is also necessary. In order to avoid repetition he has to surprise and test himself, but at the same time, this cannot be forced. Every picture is a balancing act between present and past, experience and experiment, knowledge and intuition. The artist must somehow learn something new while battening on to the old. One way of challenging himself is to experiment with a different format. Round paintings present a whole different set of problems from the reliable old rectangle. The process of painting the picture then becomes a search for new rules and relationships to discover the composition. And the painting ends up enriched by this journey of discovery.

'ROUND NUDE' Oil on Canvas

'HONG KONG GIRL' Oil on Canvas

'PUB DUBLIN' Oil on Board

'NEWSPAPER' Oil on Canvas

'BRITTANY, NUDE' *Oil on Canvas*

'PINK BED EARLY MORNING' Oil on Canvas

'BLUE LAMP' Oil on Canvas

Rooms and Windows

A key theme is stated in the window paintings - that of threshold. So much of our lives are spent on the verge of doing something, on the inside looking out (checking the weather before venturing forth, for example), that the point of change between one state and another has become of unusual importance to us. In these paintings MacKeown draws our attention to the dialogue between inside and outside, by painting the view through a window. He relishes the harsh unwavering light of summer out-of-doors, and the telling way in which it can be contrasted with diffused indoor light, which is so much kinder to flesh tones and contours.

In France, the windows open inwards, so if depicted open, achieve the sensation of bringing the countryside into the house. (The same effect would not result from the typical English outward-opening window.) This is something MacKeown particularly enjoys, for the dividing line between outside and inside is thus complicated, and the two states fruitfully interpenetrate, offering interesting visual conundra. (What is it that distinguishes outside light from interior illumination? How far does it stretch into a room? How can the patterns of nature - as glimpsed through the window - be modified by the man-made shapes of the house? These are the sort of considerations which underpin and indeed constitute MacKeown's paintings.)

A closed window presents a very different set of relationships. For instance, a green curtain to the right of a fastened wooden-framed window in the foreground of a picture encloses the spectator in the room, as if looking out. Beyond the window, in a garden, is a girl sitting reading. The two kinds of space - indoor and outdoor - are this time very separate, and their individual qualities are stressed by closing the one off from the other. A third depth of pictorial space is stated by the potted plant, placed on the windowsill outside (in effect on another plane), rendering the picture at once more complex and more satisfying.

MacKeown is a *contre-jour* painter, expert in the device of silhouetting figures against daylight. He admires the long tradition of the nude in a

'MORNING IN BRITTANY' Oil on Board

landscape and seeks to make his own contribution to it by placing the figure in an interior against a window framing a landscape setting. (Again the internal/external dialogue, with a nude perhaps drying herself by the window - a development from the related bathroom theme - clearly demonstrating that subjects for MacKeown overlap and cross-fertilize, and are not easily isolated and categorized.) Clothed figures are depicted in garden or studio settings, with or without still-life accessories. Equally he will attempt portraits or straightforward still-lifes.

In many of these interior images a woman is reading. This is of course a motif pregnant with meaning, with a history of controversy, inasmuch as the education of women is a topic that long aroused strong feelings. Such an image now functions as both symbol and record of daily existence, and it is this duality - this depth of resonance - which appeals to MacKeown. Another sub-genre consists of nudes in hotel rooms, painted all over the Celtic fringe - in Wales, Ireland and Brittany. (Does MacKeown ever paint in Cornwall?) The act of getting dressed and undressed he finds interesting, just as bath-time makes a good subject, much explored in past years.

'HOTEL, WALES' Oil on Canvas

'BATHROOM, WALES' Oil on Canvas

'LUCIE READING' Oil on Canvas

'WINDOW WITH PLANTS' Oil on Canvas

'WINDOW, SPRING LIGHT' Oil on Canvas

'NUDE NIGHT INTERIOR' Oil on Canvas

'ROOM IN THE ALPS' Oil on Board

'WEDNESDAY AFTERNOON' Oil on Canvas

'THROUGH THE WINDOW' Oil on Board

Landscape & Seascape

Landscape is another genre which MacKeown quietly investigates to good effect. He has always painted the occasional scene in his native Britain, at home or on visits to friends and family, but he has not until recently essayed the French landscape. Although it has grown increasingly familiar over the fifteen year period of his residency in Normandy, the French countryside did not initially suggest to him that deep sense of belonging which is usually felt for the country of one's birth.

Knowledge and understanding have come with the years, but there is still an element of 'foreignness' which marks out MacKeown's French landscapes. They are the work of an insider who yet remains something of an outsider (that threshold again), and this gives them an edge of detached observation which would never be found in a Frenchman painting his own soil. It is this that gives them a particular and noticeable identity (a subconscious communication, perhaps), which distinguishes them utterly from MacKeown's paintings of, for instance, Norfolk. These French scenes could not be mistaken for English pastures populated with Normandy cows. Equally, the long thin painting of a fragment of landscape outside Fishguard, the westernmost point of Wales, featuring a stone wall, a gate, a stopped car and a walking figure, could not be anywhere else than in the British Isles.

The same degree of familiarity that he needs when painting the figure is required when it comes to landscapes. In a recent painting of the local landscape, we are shown the careful gradation of fields, rising up the picture-plane from the valley below. Tall French telegraph poles make strong vertical accents, unchecked by the T top-bar of their English counterparts. They are a very useful formal device, and MacKeown may include as many as six in one landscape to articulate the space. Besides his Normandy home, which forms the subject of so many pictures,

'FIELD WITH COWS' Oil on Canvas

'THE STORM' Oil on Canvas

'GREEN FIELD' Oil on Canvas

MacKeown revisits the same few places - an odd-shaped room in the Loire valley, a house on the beach in Brittany, an island in Ireland.

The beach is an inexhaustible subject, despite the scores of beach scenes which have gone before, and the splendid achievements of such masters as Boudin or Wilson Steer. The pattern of pebbles is a rich motif to explore, in all its abstract connotations. In MacKeown's small beach paintings, a couple of figures playing in the waves at low tide suggest a poignant intimacy that approaches the poetic. The colour accents - red of spade, yellow of bucket - set up a formal dialogue which informs the whole composition, activating the picture space and heightening the emotion. There isn't really a story here - MacKeown isn't particularly interested in narrative painting - so much as a carefully constructed image of point and counterpoint, with forms echoing and answering forms. (Not surprisingly, MacKeown is very fond of Bach's counterpoint.)

'BEACH WITH WET DOGS' Oil on Canvas

'BOYS ON SUNDAY' Oil on Board

'BARLEY FIELDS' Oil on Board

'DARK COWS' Oil on Paper

'BEACH, FAMILY GROUP' Oil on Board

'BEACH TOWELS' Oil on Board

'CUT FIELDS IN NORFOLK' Oil on Canvas

'SLADE FARM IN WALES' Oil on Canvas

Techniques & Materials

MacKeown likes to make a pastel drawing of the same subject at the same time as a painting, for the one activity feeds and complements the other. Different kinds of mark-making reveal different aspects of a motif, and the way a net curtain can be drawn in pastel is quite different from the way it might be painted. Each medium has something different yet equally valid to say about the subject. In pastel there is a freshness to the colour that MacKeown values, as well as a quality of 'veiledness' which derives from the building up of the dry pigment in layers. He doesn't like 'smudged-together' pastel work, preferring to see the individual textures, hatched or scribbled on a surface.

Various degrees of unfinish are deliberate. The paint surfaces have grown thicker in recent years, and the palette more blue. Titling is a problem which holds little interest for him, and doesn't generally specify where a subject is situated. Sense of place is important to MacKeown, but it's *his* place, a private place reserved for the activity af art, not for the viewer or buyer. His signature, however, forms an important part of the painting's design. MacKeown tends to sign his pictures in red in the bottom right-hand corner, in a tone slightly lower-keyed than a red in the composition. For instance, if it was a beach painting in which a child's red spade was featured, the red of the signature would be related to that.

When he is painting in oils on board, the panels are primed with acrylic first, then with a gesso layer. But board tends to be reserved for the smaller pictures, while the bigger paintings are usually oil on canvas. MacKeown likes to experiment with media and techniques - trying out acrylic for the main body of the picture, or using a palette knife to drag the paint across the canvas, filing the blade down to make it very thin so that the texture of the paint, its physical presence, can be felt. From time to time he uses a length of bamboo to extend the brush so that he may paint at a greater distance from the canvas.

'FAMILY ON THE BEACH' Gouache on Paper

Work in the studio is essentially an editing process, deciding what to leave out. This is true whether it's a landscape or a figure painting: MacKeown likes to work both when models are present and when they're not. He works best in the early morning, and most often starts straight in painting. No preliminary drawing is done on the canvas in pencil (he only uses pencil on its own on paper). He doesn't like to mix paint and graphite in this way, nor painting and drawing, unless the drawing is on top of the paint, and done in pastel, as it then becomes part of the picture. Drawings are generally thought of as private research, not for exhibition.

MacKeown does draw on the spot quite a lot, in front of a landscape, for instance, frequently sketching with a brush in colour, and only uses photographs if he has drawn the subject first - "I have to feel it somehow", he says. He likes watching the light on a motif change from day to day, and deciding how he can best render it. He admits to using "anything I can get my hands on. But in the end I work mostly from memory." The studio process involves painting in one colour first and glazing over it, gradually getting cooler in tone. The layering is by no means even and seamless - many of MacKeown's best effects are the result of broken colour coming through from underneath.

Studio Talk

On Light. Although he paints regularly in Norfolk, he's not particularly fond of the brown light there. "I couldn't live in Switzerland - I was there for a month once - the light is Lucerne blue, and it's horrible. Here the light is soft and moist, with complimentary blues and pinks and greens - the same western Atlantic light that you get off Wales, off Ireland. You can get it in Brittany but the sea is not the same there, it's a very tough green."

MacKeown laments the stagnant state of French art, but admits that so long as he can work undisturbed, his apparent isolation is not a concern. There are always museums to visit, and rather gratifyingly the French like his work and are keen to buy it. "When I first came here I noticed that it gave me a certain distance from British art which was a great help. It let me concentrate more on what I wanted to do. I don't feel isolated in the least. I often notice that what I'm doing doesn't seem to be what everyone else is doing, but who cares? I like the fact that an artist in France is someone who has a certain place. There's a lot of respect - as an artist you aren't just someone who's a layabout on the dole, as they think in England, you're actually seen to be producing something that's of social benefit, of use to society in terms of cultural education."

He returns to England every two months to see family. These days, he tends to go to museums to see a particular picture but less and less to painting exhibitions. His remarkable photographic memory enables him to retain a painting exactly in his memory and recall it at will.

"From the moment I could walk I was dragged round museums by my father when I wasn't drawing on the floor of my grandfather's studio. Paint was all around me. The only teaching my grandfather gave me was when I was about nine drawing heads with a friend. We were arguing about how to do it. My grandfather said "you can draw them however you like, it doesn't matter". That irritated me such a lot that I've never forgotten it. Apart from that both my grandfather and my father said 'draw - keep drawing".

Who are the influential artists for him? "Degas, Whistler, Sickert I've enjoyed always. I like the way Balthus paints a lot - the construction of his pictures - though I don't like all his subjects. Ginner and Gilman I like very much, both very accomplished painters and fine draughtsmen. I love the work of Gwen John, and I think Augustus is underrated." He also admires the painter and pastellist Jean-Etienne Liotard (1702-89), whose highly realistic portraits were criticized by Horace Walpole as "too like to please", and Carel Fabritius (1622-54), Rembrandt's most gifted and original pupil, and the founder of the Delft school, who also favoured *contre-jour* compositions.

How does he select a motif? "Down on the beach today I was watching a wee child playing in the waves. That'll probably come up later in a painting. The play of light I'd have to go back and look at again. Photographs wouldn't give you that - there's a deadness to them. What interests me about Degas is that he used photographs such a lot and yet his work didn't suffer and his draughtsmanship was so strong."

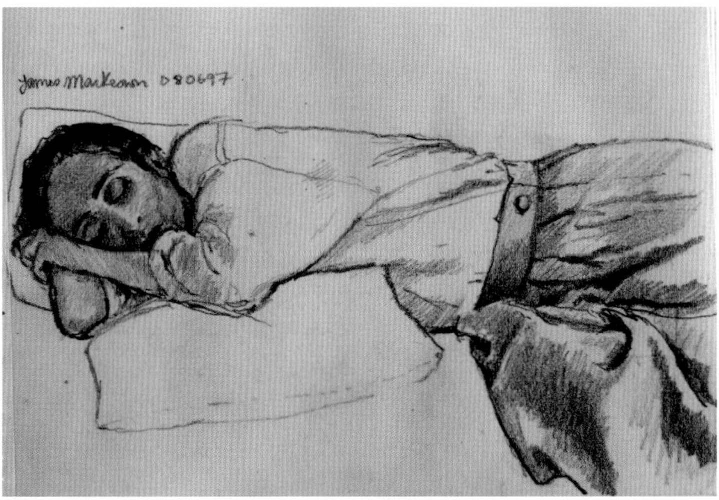

'WOMAN AT REST' Graphite on Paper

For a long time he was in awe of his grandfather, a very down-to-earth figure. "I painted my first window picture when I was 15 - a cat at a window, which I painted in Ireland with my grandfather and gave to my grandmother. That was definitely done under the influence of my grandfather, for he painted window pictures as well. Not as much as me, but one in particular called *Grey Day*, and another called *The Boys Room*, of me and my brother. He was an influence in subject, but not in terms of method."

MacKeown tends to work very fast, on more than one picture at once - a still-life, a nude, a landscape and a window painting, perhaps. His fine new studio, built off the kitchen of his home, is arranged (though not too tidily) to facilitate uninterrupted work. His routine, broken only by periods of travel, is geared to production. "I like to know the night before what I'm going to do the next day, so that I can get up and go straight into it. I like that a lot - the feeling it's organized and I've slept on it and it's OK. I usually have a canvas ready to paint, even blocked in a little bit. Then each day I bring it to a finished state so that the following day I can re-work it as a new picture, if it needs it."

But however business-like his procedures, MacKeown is all too aware of the mysterious nature of his calling. "You search for one particular thing all the time, and you can't quite reach it, and you go back and back and back. You might change the subject but you're still searching for that something. I can't quite put it into words - but perhaps it's immortality." Immortality for the paintings he is careful to make to last, or for the spirit which drives him as an artist? Both, I think.

Andrew Lambirth

'NUDE AT WINDOW' Oil and Graphite

'PORTRAIT OF MODEL' Graphite

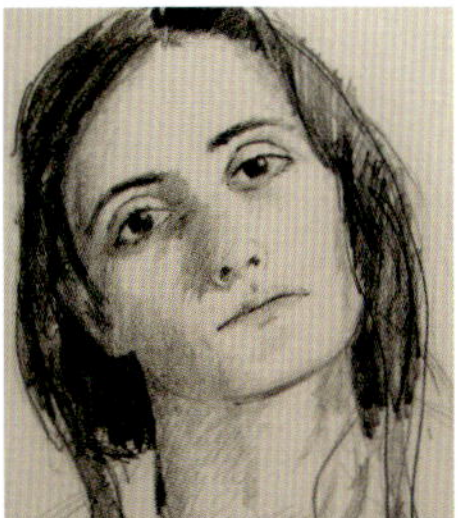

James MacKeown

Born in London 1961 of Irish origin. Spent much of childhood in Ireland, East Anglia, Turkey and Wales. Living in Normandy near Etretat since 1988 but maintaining contact with England, Ireland and Wales on a regular basis.

EXHIBITIONS

1977	Mixed show Caldwell Gallery, Belfast
	Silver Star Award at the Royal Drawing Society, Childrens Academy
1980	One man show at the Grant Gallery, Northern Ireland (and 82)
1981	Portrait highly commended at the National Portrait Gallery
1983	One man show at the Flask Gallery, Norfolk
1984	Second Norfolk show, work shown at the Phoenix Gallery, Suffolk
1985	One man show at the Sessions Gallery, Newport, Pembrokeshire
	Work shown in the Mid Wales Show
1986	Work shown by the Linfield Gallery in the Bath Festival. Work shown in the Welsh National Eisteddfod
1987	One man show at the Fermoy Arts Centre, Norfolk
	One man show at the Phoenix Gallery, Suffolk (and 88, 89, 91)
	Paintings shown in the Exhibition 'Eight British Artists' at Kingston Upon Thames
1989	One man show at the Highgate Gallery, London (and 91)
1990	Group show at the Galerie Rollin, Rouen (and 94, 96, 97, 98, 99)
	Three generations at the Highgate Gallery, London, at the Phoenix Gallery, Suffolk, at the Eakins Gallery, Belfast, at the Mistral Gallery, London
1991	Group show at the Eakins Gallery, Belfast
1992	One man show at Galerie 13, Paris
	One man show at the Eakins Gallery, Belfast
1993	One man show at the Mistral Gallery , London
	One man show at the Galerie Rollin, Rouen (and 95, 97, 99)
1994	Group show at the Mistral Gallery, London (and 95)
	One man show at Galerie Alfa, Le Havre (and 96, 98, 2000)
1995	Group shows at:
	Galerie Maig Davaud, Paris
	Adam Gallery, Bath
	West Wales Arts Centre, Fishguard (and 96, 98)
1996	Group shows at
	Bell Gallery, Belfast (and 98)
	Bank Street Gallery, Seven Oaks (and 98)
1997	One man show at the West Wales Arts Centre (and 99)
	One man show at the Bell Gallery, Belfast (and 98)

Group shows at:
Galerie Colette Dubois, Paris (and 98)
Galerie Alfa, Le Havre (and 98, 99)
Bank Street Gallery, Seven Oaks
Solomon Gallery, Dublin

1998 One man show at the Galerie Colette Dubois, Paris (and 2000)
Group shows at: Solomon Gallery, Dublin

1999 One man show at the Solomon Gallery, Dublin
One man show at the Galerie Côté Galerie, Paris
Group show at Galerie Sepia, Hong Kong'Beware French Painters'

2000 One man show at the Bell Gallery
One man show at Galerie Alfa, Le Havre
One man show at Galerie Colette Dubois, Paris
One man show at the Galerie Côté Galerie, Paris

2001 One Man shows Bruton St Gallery, London, West Wales Arts Centre, Galerie Rollin, Cote Galerie

2002 One Man Shows at the Bell Gallery, Cote Galerie, Colette Dubois, Alfa, Galerie Clement

2003 One man shows at Cote Galerie, West Wales Arts Centre, Solomon Gallery

Works on show at :

Rollin, Solomon, Bell, Bank Street, West Wales Arts Centre, Alfa Colette Dubois, Bruton Street Gallery, Edward Montgomery Fine Art USA

Work in Private Collections in:

France, Ireland, Britain, Canada, United States, Saudi Arabia, Japan, Switzerland, China, Hong Kong

Work purchased / Public collections

The Comtemporary Arts Society of Wales. The National Library of Wales Collection
The National Self Portrait Collection of Ireland. The Colas Foundation (France)

Prizes;

Silver Award at the Royal Drawing Society, 1977
Highly commended at the National Portrait Gallery Portrait Award, 1981
Winner of the Silver Medal Award at the Royal Ulster Academy, 2000 with portrait of Tom Carr